AF316681

9 reasons 2

Rewrite and Approve the Constitution via Referendum

Library of Congress Catalog
Names: Rodulfo, Juan
ISBN: 979-8-3494-0794-9 (e-book)
ISBN: 979-8-3494-0795-6 (paperback)
ISBN: 979-8-3494-0806-9 (hardcover)
First edition
Layout by Juan Rodulfo
Cover art by Guaripete Solutions
Production: Aussie Trading, LLC
books@aussietrading.ltd
Printed in the USA

*"Democracy arises out of the notion
that those who are equal in any respect are
equal in all respects; because men are equally
free, they claim to be absolutely equal."*

Aristotle

Introduction: The Case for a Fifth Wave of Reform

The United States Constitution, ratified in 1788, is the world's longest-surviving written charter of government. It is a masterpiece of 18th-century political theory, a product of Enlightenment thinking that established a framework for republican governance, individual liberties, and the rule of law. For over two centuries, it has been a symbol of stability and a beacon of democratic aspirations. Yet, its very endurance has created a paradox. The reverence with which Americans hold the document often masks its growing inadequacies in a world the framers could never have envisioned. The stability it provides has, in many respects, calcified into a rigid inflexibility that threatens the very democracy it was designed to protect.

We are living in an era of unprecedented challenges: the digital revolution, accelerating climate change, profound economic inequality, and a crisis of political polarization that has rendered our governing institutions nearly inert. The Constitution, a document written for an agrarian republic of four million people, now governs a globally interconnected nation of over 330 million. Its elegant prose on liberty and justice rings hollow when its structural mechanics fail to address the fundamental problems of our time. The system of checks and balances, once a safeguard against tyranny, has become a formula for perpetual gridlock. The rights it enumerates are fiercely debated in their application to technologies like artificial intelligence and genetic engineering. The representative democracy architecture is distorted by mechanisms like the Electoral

College and gerrymandering, which systematically disempower a majority of citizens.

This book argues that the time has come for a profound, democratic reconsideration of our founding charter. It makes the case not for a piecemeal amendment process, which has proven insufficient, nor for a partisan-driven convention of states, which risks capture by special interests, but for a national referendum. This is a call to empower the American people to debate, rewrite, and ultimately approve a constitution for the 21st century. Such a process is not a rejection of the American experiment but its ultimate fulfillment—a reaffirmation of the principle that governments derive their just powers from the consent of the governed.

The following nine Reasons will lay out the urgent reasons for this call to action. We will explore how the current framework fails to meet modern governance challenges, from digital privacy to environmental regulation. We will analyze how direct democracy can break the legislative paralysis that grips Washington. We will confront the issue of judicial overreach and how a referendum can restore popular sovereignty. Each Reason builds a cumulative case that the systemic problems we face are not merely policy failures but constitutional ones. They are bugs in the operating system of American democracy that cannot be patched with legislation alone; they require a fundamental rewrite.

This is not a call for revolution but for renewal. It is grounded in the historical understanding that the Constitution was never meant to be a sacred, unchangeable text. It has undergone four distinct waves of reform—the Founding itself, Reconstruction, the Progressive Era, and the Civil Rights Era—each prompted by a national crisis that revealed the inadequacies of the existing order. We are now in the midst of another such crisis. To ignore the need for systemic change is to risk the very foundations of the republic. By embracing a referendum, we can channel the political energy of our turbulent times into a constructive, unifying project: to form a more perfect Union, once again.

Reason 1: Modernizing Governance for 21st-Century Challenges

The year is 1787. The world is lit by candle and fire, information travels at the speed of a horse, and the primary concerns of governance revolve around agriculture, maritime trade, and the delicate balance of power between a handful of newly independent states. In this context, a group of visionary, yet mortal, men drafted the U.S. Constitution. It was a document for its time—radical, innovative, and deeply pragmatic. It established a federal system, separated powers, and laid the groundwork for a durable republic. But it was not, and could not be, a document for all time.

Today, the challenges that define our political, economic, and social landscape bear little resemblance to those of the late 18th century. We live in a world of instantaneous global communication, quantum computing, artificial intelligence, and a planetary climate system pushed to its brink. The framework designed for a pre-industrial, agrarian society is now straining under the weight of complexities its authors could not have fathomed. This foundational mismatch between our 18th-century constitution and our 21st-century reality is the first and most compelling reason for a comprehensive rewrite approved by popular referendum.

The most glaring area of inadequacy is in the realm of technology. Consider the Fourth Amendment, which protects against "unreasonable searches and seizures" and requires warrants based on probable cause. This was written in response to the physical invasion of homes by British soldiers. How does this principle apply when the "search" is the silent, invisible collection of trillions of bytes of personal data by corporations and government agencies? The Supreme Court has struggled mightily to stretch the fabric of the Fourth Amendment to cover the digital age, with landmark cases like *Carpenter v. United States* (2018) attempting to apply its protections to cell phone location data. However, these judicial patches are reactive, slow, and create a confusing and inconsistent legal landscape. The core problem remains there is no explicit, constitutionally enshrined right to digital privacy, leaving one of the most fundamental aspects of modern life vulnerable to technological and political whims. A rewritten constitution could codify this right, setting clear boundaries for state surveillance and corporate data exploitation.

Similarly, the challenge of regulating artificial intelligence exposes the limits of our current charter. Does AI-generated text, which can be used to create hyper-realistic disinformation, constitute "speech" under the First Amendment? Who is liable when an autonomous AI system causes harm? How do we protect intellectual property in an age of generative models that learn from existing human creation? These are not questions that can be adequately answered by reinterpreting the intentions of James Madison. They require a new set of foundational principles that balance innovation with accountability, principles that should be debated and decided by the people, not left to a nine-person court to divine from historical analogy. A referendum process would force a national conversation about the role we want AI to play in our society and allow us to embed those values into our governing document.

Beyond technology, the crisis of climate change presents perhaps the most existential threat and the clearest example of constitutional failure. The Constitution grants Congress the power to regulate "commerce... among the several States." This Commerce Clause has been the primary legal tool for federal environmental regulation for decades. However, its effectiveness is constantly challenged by legal battles over the scope of federal authority, leading to a patchwork of regulations that are often weakened or reversed with each new administration. The sheer scale and urgency of the climate crisis—a global problem that transcends state and national borders—demands a more explicit and powerful constitutional basis for action. Nations like

Ecuador and Bolivia have amended their constitutions to include a "right to a healthy environment" or the "rights of nature," providing a durable legal foundation for bold climate policy. A U.S. constitutional referendum could similarly empower the federal government to act decisively on climate change, insulating long-term environmental strategy from the vagaries of partisan politics and judicial activism.

The historical precedent for such fundamental updates is clear. The nation has previously faced periods of profound technological and social disruption that necessitated constitutional change. The Progressive Era (roughly 1890-1920) saw the country grappling with industrialization, urbanization, and corporate power. The problems of a nationalized economy, worker exploitation, and political corruption could not be solved by the pre-existing constitutional framework. The result was a wave of four constitutional amendments (16th through 19th) that authorized a federal income tax, established the direct election of senators, enacted prohibition, and granted women the right to vote. These were not minor tweaks; they were fundamental alterations to the structure of American governance, pushed forward by a broad-based social movement that recognized the old rules no longer applied.

We are living through a similar transformational period today. The digital revolution is as profound as the industrial revolution. The climate crisis is a challenge on par with the Civil War. To pretend that the 1787 framework is sufficient to navigate these waters is a dangerous act of denial. A constitution is not merely a historical artifact to be revered; it is the primary tool through which a society governs itself. When the tool is no longer fit for the task, it must be redesigned. A referendum is the most democratic means to achieve this, ensuring that the new design reflects the will and the wisdom of the entire nation, ready to face the challenges of the 21st century and beyond.

References for Reason 1:

- *Carpenter v. United States*, 585 U.S. ____ (2018).
- Levinson, S. (2006). *Our Undemocratic Constitution: Where the Constitution Goes Wrong (and How We the People Can Correct It)*. Oxford University Press.
- Sunstein, C. R. (2001). *Designing Democracy: What Constitutions Do*. Oxford University Press.

- Tribe, L. H. (2008). *The Invisible Constitution*. Oxford University Press.

Reason 2: Breaking Congressional Gridlock Through Direct Democracy

The United States Congress, the institution designed by the framers to be the deliberative heart of the republic, is broken. In the eyes of the American public, it has become a symbol of dysfunction, a theater of partisan warfare where urgent national problems are left to fester. Issues with broad popular support—from comprehensive immigration reform and climate action to universal background checks for gun purchases and campaign finance reform—die quiet deaths in committee, are filibustered into oblivion, or are stripped of their meaning through partisan poison pills. This is not a temporary affliction or the fault of a single political party; it is a chronic, structural disease born of our constitutional design and exacerbated by modern political realities.

The core of the problem lies in a system of checks and balances that has been weaponized in an age of hyper-partisanship. The framers envisioned a system where competing factions would compromise to achieve the common good. They did not anticipate a two-party duopoly where partisan identity would become a form of tribalism, and the primary goal of the minority party would be to ensure the majority party fails. Mechanisms like the Senate filibuster, which is not in the Constitution but is a procedural rule allowed by it, empower a small minority of senators representing a fraction of the population to block any and all legislation that does not serve their narrow political interests. The result is perpetual gridlock, where the will of the majority of Americans is consistently thwarted.

This legislative paralysis is a direct threat to democratic legitimacy. When a government is consistently unable to respond to the expressed preferences of its citizens, faith in the democratic process itself begins to erode. This creates a dangerous vacuum that can be filled by demagoguery, political apathy, or calls for authoritarian solutions. If the central representative body of a democracy cannot function, democracy itself is in peril.

This is where the second powerful argument for a constitutional referendum emerges: to provide a mechanism for the people to bypass a sclerotic legislature and enact laws directly. The concept of direct democracy is not alien to the American tradition. Many states, particularly in the West, embraced citizen-initiated referendums and initiatives during the Progressive Era as a way to combat the influence of powerful railroad and corporate monopolies over state legislatures. The "Oregon System," adopted in the early 20th century, became a model for how direct democracy could serve as a vital check on a corrupt or unresponsive representative body. It allowed citizens to propose laws, veto laws passed by the legislature, and recall elected officials.

A national referendum process, enshrined in a rewritten constitution, could serve a similar purpose on a federal scale. It could create a "safety valve" for the political system, allowing popular will to be translated into law when Congress fails to act. Imagine a system where a petition signed by a certain percentage of the electorate could place a proposed law on a national ballot. If passed by a majority of voters, it would become law, with the same force as a bill passed by Congress and signed by the president. This would not replace Congress but supplement it, forcing legislators to be more responsive to public opinion under the ever-present threat of being bypassed by the people themselves.

Skeptics of direct democracy often raise concerns about the "tyranny of the majority" and the potential for voters to be swayed by populist passions or misinformation. These are valid concerns, but they are not insurmountable. A well-designed referendum process can include crucial safeguards. For example, it could require a supermajority for passage or require that a measure pass in a certain number of states as well as nationally to ensure broad consensus. It could mandate that the text of a referendum be reviewed for constitutional consistency (against a new, clearer constitution) and that its fiscal impact be independently analyzed and widely publicized.

Moreover, the experience of other developed democracies shows that direct democracy can be a powerful tool for resolving contentious issues and breaking political deadlocks. Switzerland is the most famous example, where frequent referendums on a wide range of issues are a normal part of political life. This has not led to chaos or tyranny but to a political culture of compromise, as the government knows any law it passes can be challenged by the people. More recently, Ireland has used referendums to resolve deeply divisive social issues that had paralyzed its legislature for decades, including the legalization of same-sex marriage in 2015 and the repeal of a constitutional ban on abortion in 2018. In both cases, the referendum process sparked intense, nationwide public debate that was largely thoughtful and substantive, ultimately leading to a clear resolution that carried immense democratic legitimacy.

By embedding mechanisms for direct democracy into a rewritten constitution, we would not be abandoning the principle of representative government. Instead, we would be enhancing it, creating a system where representation is disciplined by the potential for direct citizen intervention. It would force members of Congress to look beyond their partisan silos and the demands of their wealthiest donors, and to remember that they are ultimately accountable to the American people. A referendum to approve such a system would be the ultimate expression of popular sovereignty—the people reclaiming their power to break the gridlock and make their government work for them once again.

References for Reason 2:

- Binder, S. (2015). The Dysfunctional Congress. *Annual Review of Political Science, 18*(1), 85-101.
- Gallagher, M. (2019). *The Referendum in Ireland: A Historical, Political, and Legal Analysis.* Routledge.
- Garry, J., & Pow, J. (2020). Deliberation and the referendum: The case of the Irish Citizens' Assembly on abortion. *Politics and Governance, 8*(2), 163-172.
- Smith, D. A., & Tolbert, C. J. (2004). *Educated by Initiative: The Effects of Direct Democracy on Citizens and Political Organizations in the American States.* University of Michigan Press.

Reason 3: Correcting Judicial Overreach

In the architecture of American democracy, the Supreme Court was intended to be the "least dangerous" branch, an impartial arbiter of law, not a super-legislature of robed philosophers. Yet, in recent decades, the Court has evolved into one of the most powerful and polarizing forces in American life. With lifetime appointments insulating them from public accountability, nine justices now wield the power to reshape American society on the most contentious issues, often in direct opposition to the will of the majority. This phenomenon of judicial overreach—where the Court substitutes its own policy preferences for those of elected representatives or the people themselves—has dangerously eroded public trust in the judiciary and created a compelling need for a popular check on its power. A constitutional referendum offers the most legitimate tool to achieve this recalibration.

The doctrine of judicial review, established in *Marbury v. Madison* (1803), gives the Court the authority to declare laws unconstitutional. While a crucial check on legislative and executive power, this authority was never intended to be absolute. Over time, however, the Court's interpretation of its own power has expanded dramatically. The process of judicial appointments has devolved into a bare-knuckle political brawl, where justices are selected not for their jurisprudential brilliance but for their perceived loyalty to a partisan agenda. The result is a Court that appears less like a neutral umpire and more like a team in the political game, issuing 5-4 decisions on foundational issues that track perfectly with the partisan alignment of the presidents who appointed them.

Two landmark cases epitomize this crisis. The first is *Citizens United v. Federal Election Commission* (2010), in which a narrow majority of the Court ruled that corporations have the same First Amendment free speech rights as people, striking down decades of campaign finance law. The decision opened the floodgates to unlimited corporate and union spending in elections, fundamentally altering the landscape of American politics. The ruling was, and remains, deeply unpopular with the American public, who overwhelmingly believe that money has too much influence in politics. Yet, the people have had no recourse. The decision stands as a testament to the Court's power to impose a deeply consequential and unpopular policy preference on the entire nation.

More recently, the decision in *Dobbs v. Jackson Women's Health Organization* (2022) overturned nearly fifty years of precedent established in *Roe v. Wade*, eliminating the constitutional right to abortion. Regardless of one's position on the issue, the ruling was a stark demonstration of raw judicial power. It erased a right that generations of Americans had come to rely on and threw the issue back to the states, creating a chaotic and unequal landscape of reproductive freedom. Polling consistently showed that a majority of Americans supported upholding *Roe v. Wade*. The *Dobbs* decision was a clear instance of the Court moving against popular consensus, an act that has severely damaged its legitimacy in the eyes of millions.

Historically, the American people have not been powerless in the face of judicial overreach. The Constitution itself has been amended on at least seven occasions specifically to reverse or clarify a Supreme Court decision. The Eleventh Amendment was ratified to overturn *Chisholm v. Georgia* and protect states from certain lawsuits. The Reconstruction Amendments (13th, 14th, and 15th) were a direct repudiation of the infamous *Dred Scott* decision. The Sixteenth Amendment, authorizing a federal income tax, was passed to override the Court's ruling in *Pollock v. Farmers' Loan & Trust Co.* The Twenty-Sixth Amendment, lowering the voting age to 18, reversed *Oregon v. Mitchell.* This history shows a clear, if difficult, path for popular sovereignty to have the final say.

The problem is that the modern Article V amendment process is so difficult as to be nearly impossible, especially in a time of deep partisan division. A constitutional referendum provides

34

a more direct and democratic alternative. It allows the people to bypass a captured amendment process and speak with a clear voice on issues the Court has failed to resolve in line with broad public values. A referendum could be used to codify rights that the Court has either threatened or eliminated, such as the right to privacy, reproductive freedom, or marriage equality. It could be used to pass a campaign finance amendment that explicitly states that corporations are not people and that money is not speech, effectively overturning *Citizens United.*

This is not about politicizing the Court further; it is about depoliticizing it. By giving the people a mechanism to resolve foundational questions of rights and values, we would relieve the Court of the burden of being the final arbiter of our most divisive political battles. The judiciary would be returned to its proper role: interpreting the law as written, not creating it from whole cloth. A referendum process would serve as a powerful reminder to the justices that their authority is derived from the Constitution, and that the ultimate authority to define and shape that Constitution rests not with them, but with "We the People."

References for Reason 3:

- *Citizens United v. Federal Election Commission*, 558 U.S. 310 (2010).
- *Dobbs v. Jackson Women's Health Organization*, 597 U.S. ____ (2022).
- Geyh, C. G. (2016). *When Courts & Congress Collide: The Struggle for Control of America's Judicial System.* University of Michigan Press.

- Rosen, J. (2007). *The Most Democratic Branch: How the Courts Serve America.* Oxford University Press.
- Tushnet, M. (2005). *Taking the Constitution Away from the Courts.* Princeton University Press.

Reason 4: Enhancing Democratic Legitimacy

A government's legitimacy rests on the belief of its people that its power is just and its structure is fair. In the United States, that foundational belief is cracking. Two key features of our constitutional architecture—the Electoral College and the malapportionment of the Senate—systematically distort the democratic principle of "one person, one vote." They create a system where a minority of the population can control the presidency and the legislative agenda, leading to a profound crisis of legitimacy. The outcomes of our elections and the laws passed by our Congress increasingly do not reflect the will of the American majority. To restore faith in our democracy, these anti-majoritarian institutions must be reformed, and a national referendum is the most legitimate means to do so.

The Electoral College is perhaps the most well-known and controversial of these anachronisms. Conceived as a compromise between electing the president by popular vote and electing the president by a vote in Congress, it was also a concession to slave states, whose enslaved populations inflated their representation through the Three-Fifths Compromise. Today, it has resulted in two of the last four presidents taking office despite losing the national popular vote (in 2000 and 2016). This is a democratic absurdity. The fact that a voter in Wyoming has significantly more say in choosing the president than a voter in California is fundamentally unfair and breeds deep resentment. It turns presidential campaigns into a frantic dash to win a handful of "swing states," while the vast majority of the country is ignored.

Equally problematic, though less discussed, is the severe malapportionment of the U.S. Senate. The Constitution grants every state two senators, regardless of population. This was another compromise to protect the interests of small states. But today, it has created a staggering representational imbalance. California, with a population of nearly 40 million, has the same number of senators as Wyoming, with a population under 600,000. This means that a senator from Wyoming represents roughly 68 times fewer people than a senator from California. As a result, a coalition of senators representing a small fraction of the U.S. population can command a majority in the Senate, confirming judges, setting the legislative agenda, and blocking bills supported by the overwhelming majority of Americans. This is not the "cooling saucer" of deliberation the framers envisioned; it is a chokehold on democracy.

These institutions create what political scientists call a "counter-majoritarian difficulty," but for the average citizen, it feels more like a rigged system. When the government's actions consistently diverge from public opinion on issues like gun control, climate change, and healthcare, it is often because these structures allow a minority to impose its will. This erodes institutional credibility and trust, the essential glue that holds a diverse society together.

Reforming these systems through the traditional amendment process is a virtual impossibility, as it would require the very small states that benefit from the status quo to vote against their own disproportionate power. This is where a national referendum becomes essential. It provides a pathway for the national majority to enact reforms that would make our system more genuinely democratic. Proposals like the National Popular Vote Interstate Compact, an agreement among states to award their electoral votes to the candidate who wins the national popular vote, have gained traction but face immense political and legal hurdles. A referendum could bypass these obstacles and establish a national popular vote for the presidency directly.

For the Senate, a referendum could propose a variety of reforms, from amending the apportionment formula to give more populous states more senators, to abolishing the Senate in favor of a unicameral legislature, as is common in many modern democracies. While radical, such ideas deserve a national debate. A less drastic reform could involve replacing the Senate with a body elected through a system of proportional representation, where the percentage of seats a party gets is proportional to the percentage of the national vote it receives. This would ensure that all political viewpoints are represented more fairly in the legislature.

International examples prove that such fundamental reforms are possible. After decades of political stalemate and violence, Colombia used a binding, citizen-initiated referendum in 1991 as part of a process to write a new constitution that broke the grip of a two-party political elite and introduced new democratic mechanisms. The direct approval of the new charter by the people gave it a powerful legitimacy that allowed for deep structural changes to take place.

By putting reforms like the abolition of the Electoral College or the restructuring of the Senate to a national vote, we would be engaging in the ultimate act of democratic self-correction. It would not be about punishing small states, but about reaffirming the core American principle that in a democracy, the will of the people should prevail. The direct approval of such changes by a majority of Americans would lend them an unassailable legitimacy, healing the deep-seated resentment that our current system fosters and renewing the promise of a government of the people, by the people, and for the people.

References for Reason 4:

- Dahl, R. A. (2002). *How Democratic Is the American Constitution?* Yale University Press.

- Edwards III, G. C. (2011). *Why the Electoral College is Bad for America.* Yale University Press.

- Levitsky, S., & Ziblatt, D. (2018). *How Democracies Die.* Crown.

- Moyn, S. (2021). The counter-majoritarian difficulty in a new key. *Boston University Law Review, 101,* 1857-1870.

Reason 5: Addressing Systemic Inequities

The U.S. Constitution begins with the soaring phrase, "We the People," yet the document it introduces was written by and for a very specific, and exclusive, group of people: white, male property owners. It is a document whose original text protected the institution of slavery, denied women a political voice, and ignored the existence of Indigenous nations. While subsequent amendments have heroically chipped away at this exclusionary foundation, the ghost of that original sin still haunts the structure of American society. Deep-seated racial, gender, and economic disparities are not just policy failures; they are the legacy of a constitutional framework that was not designed for universal equality. To build a truly equitable nation, we must go beyond interpretation and amendment; we must rewrite the foundation itself, and a referendum is the only way to ensure the new foundation is built by all the people.

The history of constitutional reform is, in large part, the story of the struggle to expand the definition of "We the People." The Thirteenth, Fourteenth, and Fifteenth Amendments, forged in the crucible of the Civil War, abolished slavery, established birthright citizenship, and promised equal protection and voting rights to Black men. The Nineteenth Amendment, won after a century of struggle, extended suffrage to women. These were monumental achievements. Yet, for every step forward, the Constitution's structural limitations allowed for massive resistance and backlash. The promise of the Fourteenth Amendment was systematically dismantled by Jim Crow laws, upheld by a

Supreme Court that read equality out of the "equal protection" clause. Women gained the vote but continued to face legal and economic discrimination, a reality that gave rise to the decades-long, and still unfinished, fight for an Equal Rights Amendment (ERA).

The revival of the ERA, with three states ratifying it in recent years to finally meet the original threshold, demonstrates the powerful grassroots demand for explicit constitutional guarantees of equity. Yet its fate remains tied up in legal and political battles over a long-expired deadline, a perfect example of how our rigid constitutional structure impedes even widely supported progress. The demand for justice cannot wait for arcane procedural debates to conclude.

Today, the inequities are stark. Black Americans face systemic disadvantages in housing, education, employment, and the criminal justice system. The gender pay gap persists. Economic inequality has reached levels not seen since the Gilded Age, with a tiny fraction of the population controlling a vast share of the nation's wealth. These are not the random outcomes of a fair system; they are the predictable results of a system that has never fully confronted its exclusionary origins.

A constitutional referendum provides a historic opportunity to correct this. Instead of fighting state by state for piecemeal policies, we could have a national conversation about what rights and protections should be guaranteed to every American. A rewritten constitution could finally and explicitly include an Equal Rights Amendment, stating unequivocally that equality of rights under the law shall not be denied or abridged on account of sex. It could go further, enshrining protections against discrimination based on race, religion, sexual orientation, gender identity, and disability in clear, unambiguous language.

Beyond anti-discrimination principles, a 21st-century constitution could address the economic dimension of equity. Many modern constitutions around the world recognize "social and economic rights," such as the right to housing, healthcare, education, and a clean environment. While critics in the U.S. often dismiss these as unenforceable aspirations, their inclusion in a constitution serves a powerful purpose. It establishes a national commitment and provides a legal basis for citizens to hold their government accountable for ensuring a basic standard of living for everyone. A referendum could propose codifying a right to quality public education, a right to affordable healthcare, or a right to clean air and water. These are not radical ideas; they are mainstream values in most developed nations and enjoy broad support among the American people.

Enshrining these principles in a new constitution would represent a fundamental shift, moving from a framework that primarily protects people *from* government overreach to one that also defines what people have a right to expect *from* their government. It would be a declaration that true liberty is not merely the absence of tyranny but the presence of opportunity. It would transform the Constitution from a document that had to be forced to accommodate the demands of marginalized groups into a document that is, from its very inception, a charter of universal freedom and equity. Such a transformation cannot be handed down by courts or bestowed by politicians. To be legitimate and lasting, it must be authored by the people themselves, in all their diversity, through a national referendum.

References for Reason 5:

- Foner, E. (2019). *The Second Founding: How the Civil War and Reconstruction Remade the Constitution*. W. W. Norton & Company.
- Kendi, I. X. (2019). *How to Be an Antiracist*. One World.
- Piketty, T. (2014). *Capital in the Twenty-First Century*. Harvard University Press.

- Suk, J. C. (2020). *We the Women: The Unstoppable Mothers of the Equal Rights Amendment.* Simon & Schuster.

Reason 6: Preventing Authoritarian Backsliding

Democracy is not a birthright; it is a practice, and its institutions are only as strong as the norms and rules that uphold them. In recent years, the world has witnessed a trend of "authoritarian backsliding," where established democracies are eroded from within by leaders who exploit constitutional loopholes, shatter long-standing norms, and concentrate power in the executive branch. The United States is not immune to this global trend. The immense power vested in the presidency, combined with the erosion of congressional oversight and the politicization of the justice system, has created fertile ground for authoritarianism. To safeguard the future of the republic, we must hardwire our democratic defenses into the

Constitution itself, and a referendum is the safest and most legitimate way to do so.

The modern American presidency has become a dangerously powerful institution, far exceeding the vision of the framers. Through the expansive use of executive orders, declarations of national emergency, and control over the vast administrative state, presidents of both parties have steadily accumulated authority at the expense of Congress. This "imperial presidency," a term coined by historian Arthur M. Schlesinger Jr., has reached a crisis point. We have seen presidents launch military actions without clear congressional approval, redirect funds appropriated by Congress for their own purposes, and use the rhetoric of "enemy of the people" to attack the free press and the judiciary.

These actions are often technically legal, exploiting ambiguities in the Constitution and a web of statutes passed over decades. They rely on the violation of unwritten norms—traditions of restraint, respect for the other branches, and a commitment to the rule of law—that have been the guardrails of American democracy. But as we have learned, norms are fragile. They are no match for a leader determined to break them. To prevent authoritarian backsliding, we can no longer rely on tradition and goodwill. We must codify these guardrails into constitutional law.

A constitutional referendum could propose a suite of anti-authoritarian amendments. These could include clear, strict limits on the president's power to declare a national emergency and to use emergency powers without immediate congressional authorization. It could fortify congressional oversight by explicitly granting Congress the power to enforce its subpoenas against the executive branch. It could establish an independent federal ethics commission with constitutional authority to investigate and sanction corruption in all three branches of government, insulating it from political interference.

Furthermore, a referendum could address the issue of term limits. While the presidency is limited to two terms, there are no such limits for members of Congress or Supreme Court justices. This has created a permanent political class in Washington, often out of touch with the rest of the country, and has led to the current situation of lifetime judicial appointments becoming high-stakes political battles for ideological control of the Court. A constitutional referendum could propose term limits for both House and Senate members, as well as replacing lifetime judicial appointments with a single, long term (such as 18 years), which would depoliticize the confirmation process and ensure that every president has an equal number of appointments to the Court.

It is crucial to contrast this approach with the alternative method of constitutional change being pushed by some: a "Convention of States" under Article V. While theoretically a valid process, a convention called in our current hyper-partisan environment would be extraordinarily dangerous. It would be an unaccountable body, potentially captured by well-funded special interests and partisan extremists, with the power to rewrite the entire Constitution from scratch without a clear public mandate. It risks opening a Pandora's box of radical changes that could weaken, rather than strengthen, our democracy.

A referendum-driven process is the superior alternative. It is transparent, deliberative, and democratic. Instead of a closed-door convention, specific proposals would be debated openly across the country. Every voter would have a direct say in approving or rejecting these new safeguards. The process would be controlled by the people, not by a small group of delegates. It would allow us to channel the legitimate public anger at government dysfunction and corruption into a constructive project of democratic renewal, rather than risking a partisan free-for-all.

The threat of authoritarianism is real. It is not a partisan issue but a structural one. Protecting our democracy requires more than just winning the next election; it requires fortifying the democratic institutions themselves. We must repair the constitutional fences that are meant to constrain executive power and ensure accountability. A popular referendum is the people's tool to do that work, ensuring that the government remains a servant of the people, not its master.

References for Reason 6:

- Ginsburg, T., & Huq, A. Z. (2018). *How to Save a Constitutional Democracy*. University of Chicago Press.
- Levitsky, S., & Ziblatt, D. (2018). *How Democracies Die*. Crown.
- Schlesinger Jr., A. M. (2004). *The Imperial Presidency*. Houghton Mifflin Harcourt.

- Warshaw, S. A. (2015). *The Taming of the Presidency: The Limits of Executive Power*. Routledge.

Reason 7: Global Lessons in Constitutional Innovation

American constitutionalism has long been defined by a sense of exceptionalism—a belief that our 1787 charter is a singular achievement, a model to be exported, but not one that needs to learn from others. This insularity is no longer tenable. While the U.S. Constitution has grown rigid and difficult to change, nations around the world have been experimenting with innovative, participatory, and adaptive methods of constitutional design. From South Africa to Iceland, and across Latin America, countries are proving that constitutions can be living documents, not just revered relics. To build a more resilient and responsive democracy, the United States must shed its exceptionalism and draw upon these global lessons in constitutional innovation. A referendum is the key to unlocking this potential.

One of the most powerful lessons comes from post-apartheid South Africa. After the fall of the racist apartheid regime, the country embarked on one of the most inclusive constitution-making processes in history. It was not a closed-door affair for elites. The process involved a massive public participation campaign, with millions of submissions from ordinary citizens, civic organizations, and political parties. The final text, adopted in 1996, is considered one of the most progressive in the world. It includes not only traditional political rights but also a wide array of socioeconomic rights, such as the right to housing, healthcare, and education. It established powerful independent institutions to protect democracy, including a Public Protector and a

Constitutional Court. The legitimacy of the South African constitution flows directly from the fact that the people see it as their own.

Another key innovation is the idea of making constitutions more adaptable. The U.S. Constitution's Article V amendment process is notoriously difficult, requiring a two-thirds vote in both houses of Congress and ratification by three-fourths of the states. This high bar was intended to ensure stability, but it has resulted in paralysis. In contrast, other countries have built mechanisms for change and review into their charters. The constitution of Bolivia, rewritten through a participatory process and approved by referendum in 2009, contains provisions that allow for citizen-initiated reforms. The constitution of Ecuador, approved by referendum in 2008, famously includes the "rights of nature," a groundbreaking legal concept that grants ecosystems the legal right to exist and flourish, a concept born from Indigenous worldviews and modern environmental science.

Perhaps the most radical and inspiring recent example is Iceland's attempt at a crowdsourced constitution. Following the 2008 financial crisis, which shattered public trust in the country's political elite, Iceland embarked on a remarkable experiment. A randomly selected National Assembly of 950 citizens identified core principles for a new constitution. A 25-member Constitutional Council, elected by the public, then drafted a new charter, using social media like Facebook and Twitter to solicit feedback and suggestions from the entire population. While the final adoption of the draft was ultimately blocked by political elites in parliament, the process itself stands as a powerful testament to the potential of technology and direct democracy to create a truly 21st-century constitution-making process.

What can the United States learn from these examples? First, inclusivity matters. A process that genuinely engages all segments of society, especially those historically marginalized, produces a more legitimate and just outcome. Second, adaptability is a strength, not a weakness. A modern constitution should have built-in mechanisms for periodic review and reform, ensuring it can evolve with the society it governs, rather than relying solely on judicial reinterpretation or near-impossible amendment. A new U.S. constitution could, for example, mandate a popular referendum every 20 or 25 years to consider proposed revisions.

A national referendum to rewrite and approve our own constitution would be the American way of embracing these global lessons. It would be a recognition that we are part of a global community of democracies, all grappling with the challenges of modernity. It would allow us to debate and potentially adopt innovative ideas like socioeconomic rights, stronger environmental protections, or new mechanisms for democratic participation. It would break the intellectual stranglehold of "originalism"—the backward-looking ideology that insists we are bound forever by the specific intentions of 18th-century men—and free us to think creatively about the future. By looking outward, we can find the tools to rebuild our democracy from within, creating a constitution that is not just for Americans, but a renewed model for the world.

References for Reason 7:

- Dixon, R., & Ginsburg, T. (Eds.). (2011). *Comparative Constitutional Law.* Edward Elgar Publishing.

- Elkins, Z., Ginsburg, T., & Melton, J. (2009). *The Endurance of National Constitutions.* Cambridge University Press.

- Landemore, H. (2020). *Open Democracy: Reinventing Popular Rule for the Twenty-First Century.* Princeton University Press.

- Sachs, A. (2011). *The Strange Alchemy of Life and Law.* Oxford University Press.

Reason 8: Civic Engagement and Political Education

American democracy is suffering from a crisis of participation. Voter turnout is low, trust in government is at historic lows, and public discourse is poisoned by misinformation and partisan animosity. Many citizens feel alienated from the political process, viewing it as a distant and corrupt game with no relevance to their daily lives. A constitutional referendum is more than just a mechanism for legal change; it is a powerful antidote to this civic decay. The very process of debating, rewriting, and voting on our nation's foundational document would spark an unprecedented national seminar in civics, revitalizing public engagement and fostering a more informed and empowered citizenry.

The transformative power of a referendum lies in its ability to focus the national consciousness. It elevates a debate above the day-to-day noise of partisan politics and asks citizens to consider fundamental questions: What is the purpose of government? What rights should be guaranteed to all people? How should we share power and resources? How do we build a just and equitable society? These are not questions with easy answers, and forcing ourselves to grapple with them is the essence of democratic citizenship.

The experience of Ireland provides a compelling case study. In 2015 and 2018, the country held referendums to legalize same-sex marriage and repeal its constitutional ban on abortion, respectively. Both issues were deeply emotional and had divided the nation for decades. The referendum campaigns sparked months of intense, widespread, and remarkably substantive public debate. People talked about it at home, at work, and in their communities. Citizen-led organizations on both sides went door-to-door, not just to persuade, but to listen and to engage in genuine conversation. The media provided extensive coverage, and a government-established Citizens' Assembly provided a model for informed, deliberative democracy. The result was not only legal change but also a profound social and civic transformation. People felt empowered, engaged, and invested in the outcome. The referendums did not tear the country apart; they fostered a new level of political maturity and accountability.

A constitutional referendum in the United States would have a similar, if not greater, effect. It would necessitate a massive public education campaign. Schools and universities would develop curricula around the process. Civic organizations, from the League of Women Voters to local community groups, would host town halls and debates. Media organizations would have a responsibility to move beyond horse-race political coverage and provide deep, explanatory journalism about the core issues at stake.

Of course, a key challenge would be countering the tide of misinformation and disinformation that would inevitably be deployed by those who benefit from the status quo. A well-designed process would need to anticipate this. It could include the creation of an independent, non-partisan commission tasked with producing and distributing an official voter guide, which would lay out the arguments for and against the proposed changes in clear, neutral language. Publicly funded media campaigns could be used to promote this guide and direct citizens to reliable sources of information. The use of Citizens' Assemblies, like in Ireland, where a randomly selected group of citizens hears from experts and deliberates on the issues before making recommendations, could also be a powerful tool for generating informed and trusted guidance for the wider public.

The process of a referendum would, by its nature, force accountability. Politicians could not hide behind procedural tricks or partisan talking points. They would be forced to take a clear stand on the foundational principles of our democracy and defend that stand to their constituents. It would also empower citizens. The act of voting in a referendum is a direct expression of popular sovereignty, a reminder that the ultimate power lies with the people. This sense of agency is a powerful antidote to the cynicism and apathy that currently plague our politics.

Ultimately, the greatest benefit of a constitutional referendum might be the process itself. It would be a shared national project, a moment for Americans of all backgrounds and beliefs to step back from their partisan corners and engage in a conversation about their common future. It would be a chance to renew our understanding of the Constitution, not as a sacred text to be worshipped, but as our collective agreement on how we wish to govern ourselves. In an age of division and alienation, such a process could be the very thing that reminds us of our shared identity as citizens of a democratic republic.

References for Reason 8:

- Dalton, R. J. (2017). *The Participation Gap: Social Status and Political Inequality.* Oxford University Press.
- Fishkin, J. S. (2018). *Democracy When the People Are Thinking: Revitalizing Our Politics Through Public Deliberation.* Oxford University Press.
- Putnam, R. D. (2000). *Bowling Alone: The Collapse and Revival of American Community.* Simon & Schuster.
- Surowiecki, J. (2004). *The Wisdom of Crowds.* Doubleday.

Reason 9: Historical Momentum for a Fifth Wave of Reform

History does not repeat itself, but it often rhymes. The current American political moment—characterized by deep polarization, soaring economic inequality, rapid technological change, and a profound loss of faith in institutions—is not without precedent. American history can be read as a series of long periods of relative stability punctuated by intense, transformative crises that force a fundamental rethinking of the nation's constitutional order. We have experienced at least four such waves of reform. The evidence suggests we are now living at the precipice of a fifth, and a referendum-driven process is the most democratic way to channel the immense energy of this moment into systemic renewal rather than societal collapse.

The first wave was the Founding itself. The Articles of Confederation proved unworkable, leading to a crisis of governance that culminated in the Constitutional Convention of 1787 and the subsequent ratification of the new Constitution and the Bill of Rights. This was a radical rewrite, a response to a clear and present failure of the existing system.

The second wave was Reconstruction. The existential crisis of the Civil War, fought over the nation's original sin of slavery, necessitated a "second founding." The Thirteenth, Fourteenth, and Fifteenth Amendments were not mere tweaks; they were a revolutionary attempt to remake the nation on a foundation of multiracial democracy and national citizenship, fundamentally altering the relationship between the federal government, the states, and the individual.

The third wave was the Progressive Era. The Gilded Age of the late 19th century created a crisis of industrial capitalism, with massive corporate trusts, brutal labor conditions, and widespread political corruption. The existing constitutional framework was ill-equipped to handle a nationalized, industrial economy. The resulting social and political movements led to a flurry of four amendments between 1913 and 1920—the federal income tax (16th), direct election of senators (17th), Prohibition (18th), and women's suffrage (19th)—that dramatically expanded the power of the federal government and the scope of American democracy.

The fourth wave can be seen in the wake of the Great Depression and World War II, culminating in the Civil Rights Era. The economic collapse of the 1930s led to the New Deal and a radical reinterpretation of the Commerce Clause, solidifying federal power over the economy. The moral and geopolitical pressures of the Cold War, combined with the tireless struggle of the Civil Rights Movement, led to further constitutional changes, including the 24th Amendment abolishing poll taxes and the landmark civil rights and voting rights legislation that finally began to fulfill the promises of Reconstruction.

Each of these waves was precipitated by a period where the existing constitutional order proved incapable of addressing the nation's most pressing problems. The parallels to our current era are undeniable. The economic inequality of our time rivals that of the Gilded Age. The political polarization and social divisions echo the periods before the Civil War and during the turbulent 1960s. The digital revolution is as disruptive as the industrial revolution. Our political institutions are as gridlocked and unresponsive as they were before the Progressive Era reforms.

We are living in a moment of constitutional crisis, whether we choose to name it or not. The historical pattern suggests that such moments are resolved in one of two ways: through fundamental, often wrenching, reform, or through decline and disintegration. The energy for change is already present. We see it in the grassroots movements for racial justice, climate action, and gun control. We see it in the populist anger on both the left and the right, a clear sign of widespread dissatisfaction with the status quo.

The question is how this energy will be channeled. Will it be through the chaotic and dangerous path of a partisan Convention of States? Will it be through continued political violence and delegitimization? Or will it be through a structured, peaceful, and democratic process of renewal?

A national referendum to rewrite and approve the Constitution offers the most promising path forward. It acknowledges the historical gravity of our moment and provides a mechanism equal to the scale of our challenges. It takes the accumulated frustrations and aspirations of the American people and directs them toward a common project. It is an embrace of the long American tradition of periodically remaking ourselves in response to crisis. A referendum would not be a rejection of our history, but the next logical Reason in it—a fifth wave of reform to create a more perfect union, guided by the principle that has powered every previous wave of change: the sovereign will of the people.

References for Reason 9:

- Ackerman, B. (1991). *We the People, Volume 1: Foundations.* Harvard University Press.

- Foner, E. (2019). *The Second Founding: How the Civil War and Reconstruction Remade the Constitution.* W. W. Norton & Company.

- Hofstadter, R. (1955). *The Age of Reform: From Bryan to F.D.R.* Alfred A. Knopf.

- Wood, G. S. (2009). *Empire of Liberty: A History of the Early Republic, 1789-1815.* Oxford University Press.

Conclusion: A More Perfect Union by the People's Will

The United States Constitution is a paradox. It is both a monumental achievement of democratic thought and a relic of a bygone era. It is the source of our stability and the cause of our paralysis. For too long, we have treated it as a sacred text, a finished work to be interpreted by a priestly class of judges, rather than as what it is: our collective agreement on how we choose to govern ourselves, an agreement that can, and must, be updated when it no longer serves its purpose.

This book has laid out nine urgent reasons why that time is now. We have seen how our 18th-century framework is failing to meet the challenges of the 21st, from AI to climate change. We have examined how structural flaws like the filibuster and Senate malapportionment have created a crisis of legislative gridlock and democratic illegitimacy. We have confronted the reality of a judiciary that has become a source of political power rather than impartial justice, and a system that perpetuates the deep inequities of race, gender, and class upon which it was partly founded. We have explored the rising threat of authoritarianism and the need for new constitutional guardrails.

But this book has not been a portrait of despair. It has been a call to action, grounded in a profound faith in the democratic potential of the American people. For each problem, we have seen a solution rooted in the principle of popular sovereignty. We have drawn lessons from global innovations in constitutional design and recognized the immense power of a referendum process to revitalize civic education and participation. Finally, we have placed our current struggles within the grand sweep of American history, identifying the powerful momentum for a fifth great wave of constitutional reform.

The proposal for a national referendum to rewrite and approve our Constitution is not a radical break from the American tradition. It is the deepest expression of it. It is a return to the spirit of 1776 and 1787, a reaffirmation that governments are instituted among people to secure their rights and derive their just powers from the consent of the governed. When a government becomes destructive of these ends, it is the right of the people to alter or to abolish it, and to institute a new government.

This is not a call to abolish our government, but to alter it, to renew it, to make it worthy of the challenges and aspirations of our time. It is a formidable task, fraught with difficulty and risk. But the risk of inaction—of allowing our democracy to slowly crumble under the weight of its own contradictions—is far greater.

To embark on this path requires courage, imagination, and a willingness to trust our fellow citizens. It requires us to believe, as the framers did, that ordinary people are capable of extraordinary acts of self-governance. The journey toward a more perfect union is never-ending. This is our generation's moment to take up that work, to engage in the great, messy, and glorious task of democratic deliberation, and to create, by the people's will, a constitution that can secure the blessings of liberty for ourselves and our posterity.

Juan Ramon Rodulfo Moya, **Defined by Nature**: Inhabitant of Planet Earth, Human, Son of Eladio Rodulfo and Briceida Moya, Brother of Gabriela, Gustavo and Katiuska, Father of Gabriel and Sofia; **Defined by society**: Venezuelan Citizen (Limited Human Rights by default), Friend of many, enemy of few, Neighbor, Student/Teacher/Student, Worker/Supervisor/Manager/Leader/Worker, Husband of K/Ex-Husband of K/Husband of Y; **Defined by the U.S. Immigration Office**: Legal Alien; **Classroom studies**: Master's Degree in Human Resource Management, English, Mandarin Chinese; **Real-World Studies**: Human Behavior; **Home Studios**: SEO Webmaster, Graphic Design, Application and Website Development, Internet and Social Media Marketing, Video Production, YouTube Branding, Part 107 Commercial Drone Pilot, Import-Export, Affiliate Marketing, Cooking, Laundry, Home Cleaning; **Work experience**: Public-Private-Entrepreneurial Sectors; **Other definitions:** Bitcoin Evangelist, Human Rights, Peace and Love Advocate.

Publications:

Books:

Why Maslow? How to use his theory to stay in Power Forever (2018)

¿Por qué Maslow? Cómo usar su teoría para permanecer en el Poder por siempre (2018)

Asylum Seekers (2018)

En busca de Asilo (2018)

Manual for Gorillas: 9 Rules to be the "FER-PECT" dictator (2019)

Manual para Gorilas: 9 Reglas para ser el dictador "FER-PECTO" (2019)

Why you must Play the Lottery (2019)

Por qué debes jugar la Lotería (2021)

Para Español Oprima #2: Speaking Spanish in Times of Xenophobia (2019)

Cause of Death: IGNORANCE, Human Behavior in Times of PANIC (2019)

Politics explained for Millennials, GENs XYZ and future generations (2022)

Política explicada para Millennials, GENs xyz y futuras generaciones (2022)

Las cenizas del Ejército Libertador (2023)

Remain Silent: The only right we have. The legal Aliens (2023)

9 Reasons 2 make fair trial a constitutional right (2025)

9 Reasons 2 make freedom from slavery torture and discrimination constitutional rights (2025)

9 Reasons 2 make healthcare and adequate standard of living constitutional rights (2025)

9 Reasons 2 make freedom of speech religion and association constitutional rights (2025)

9 Reasons 2 make housing a constitutional right (2025)

9 Reasons 2 humanize audit and make public the incarceration system (2025)

9 Reasons 2 overhauling the IRS to tax big fishes (2025)

9 Reasons 2 replace oaths on bibles by legal contracts (2025)

9 Reasons 2 make life liberty and security constitutional rights (2025)

9 Reasons 2 make voting mandatory (2025)

9 Reasons 2 legalize marihuana (2025)

9 Reasons 2 make marriage a private issue (2025)

9 Reasons 2 replace the presidential system by a parliamentary system in the US (2025)

9 Reasons 2 pay $500 for voting (2025)

9 Reasons 2 legalize sex work (2025)

9 Reasons 2 rewrite and approve the constitution via referendum (2025)

9 Reasons 2 eliminate speed limits and traffic stops (2025)

9 Reasons 2 modernizing the supreme court (2025)

9 Reasons 2 tax churches (2025)

9 Reasons 2 make unionization a constitutional right (2025)

9 Reasons 2 make universal basic income a constitutional right (2025)

9 Reasons 2 make indexed wages a constitutional right (2025)

9 Reasons 2 modernizing the TSA (2025)

9 Reasons 2 stop the use of prefixes to call Americans (2025)

Self-made billionaire in the US, Girl, hold my beer (2025)

BLOGS:

Noticias de Nueva Esparta, Ubuntu Café, Coffee Secrets, Guaripete Pro, Rodulfox, Red Wasp Drone, Barista Pro, Gorila Travel, Fortune Cookie Coach, All Books, Vicky Toys.

Audiovisual Productions:

PODCASTS:

Ubuntu Cafe | Vicky Erotic Tales | Fortune Cookie Coach | All Books, available at: juanrodulfo.com/podcasts

MUSIC:

Albums: Margarita | Race to Extinction | Relaxed Panda | Amazonia | Cassiopeia | Caracas | Arcoiris Musical | Close Your Eyes, available at: juanrodulfo.com/music

PHOTOGRAPHY & VIDEO:

On sale at Adobe Stock, iStock, Shutterstock, and Veectezy, available at: juanrodulfo.com/gallery

Social Media Profiles:

BlueSky / Twitter / FB / Instagram / TikTok/ VK / LinkedIn / Sina Weibo: @rodulfox

Google Author: https://g.co/kgs/grjtN5
Google Artist: https://g.co/kgs/H7Fiqg
Twitter: https://twitter.com/rodulfox
Facebook: https://facebook.com/rodulfox
LinkedIn: https://www.linkedin.com/in/rodulfox
Instagram: https://www.instagram.com/rodulfox/
VK: https://vk.com/rodulfox
TikTok: https://www.tiktok.com/@rodulfox

Trading
View: https://www.tradingview.com/u/rodulfo
x/

Table of Contents

96

Comprehensive Bibliography

Ackerman, B. (1991). *We the People, Volume 1: Foundations*. Harvard University Press.

Binder, S. (2015). The Dysfunctional Congress. *Annual Review of Political Science, 18*(1), 85-101.

Carpenter v. United States, 585 U.S. ____ (2018).

Citizens United v. Federal Election Commission, 558 U.S. 310 (2010).

Dahl, R. A. (2002). *How Democratic Is the American Constitution?* Yale University Press.

Dalton, R. J. (2017). *The Participation Gap: Social Status and Political Inequality*. Oxford University Press.

Dixon, R., & Ginsburg, T. (Eds.). (2011). *Comparative Constitutional Law*. Edward Elgar Publishing.

Dobbs v. Jackson Women's Health Organization, 597 U.S. ____ (2022).

Edwards III, G. C. (2011). *Why the Electoral College is Bad for America*. Yale University Press.

Elkins, Z., Ginsburg, T., & Melton, J. (2009). *The Endurance of National Constitutions*. Cambridge University Press.

Fishkin, J. S. (2018). *Democracy When the People Are Thinking: Revitalizing Our Politics Through Public Deliberation*. Oxford University Press.

Foner, E. (2019). *The Second Founding: How the Civil War and Reconstruction Remade the Constitution*. W. W. Norton & Company.

Gallagher, M. (2019). *The Referendum in Ireland: A Historical, Political, and Legal Analysis*. Routledge.

Garry, J., & Pow, J. (2020). Deliberation and the referendum: The case of the Irish Citizens' Assembly on abortion. *Politics and Governance, 8*(2), 163-172.

Geyh, C. G. (2016). *When Courts & Congress Collide: The Struggle for Control of America's Judicial System.* University of Michigan Press.

Ginsburg, T., & Huq, A. Z. (2018). *How to Save a Constitutional Democracy.* University of Chicago Press.

Hofstadter, R. (1955). *The Age of Reform: From Bryan to F.D.R.* Alfred A. Knopf.

Kendi, I. X. (2019). *How to Be an Antiracist.* One World.

Landemore, H. (2020). *Open Democracy: Reinventing Popular Rule for the Twenty-First Century.* Princeton University Press.

Levinson, S. (2006). *Our Undemocratic Constitution: Where the Constitution Goes Wrong (and How We the People Can Correct It).* Oxford University Press.

Levitsky, S., & Ziblatt, D. (2018). *How Democracies Die.* Crown.

Moyn, S. (2021). The counter-majoritarian difficulty in a new key. *Boston University Law Review, 101*, 1857-1870.

Piketty, T. (2014). *Capital in the Twenty-First Century*. Harvard University Press.

Putnam, R. D. (2000). *Bowling Alone: The Collapse and Revival of American Community*. Simon & Schuster.

Rosen, J. (2007). *The Most Democratic Branch: How the Courts Serve America*. Oxford University Press.

Sachs, A. (2011). *The Strange Alchemy of Life and Law*. Oxford University Press.

Schlesinger Jr., A. M. (2004). *The Imperial Presidency*. Houghton Mifflin Harcourt.

Smith, D. A., & Tolbert, C. J. (2004). *Educated by Initiative: The Effects of Direct Democracy on Citizens and Political Organizations in the American States*. University of Michigan Press.

Suk, J. C. (2020). *We the Women: The Unstoppable Mothers of the Equal Rights Amendment*. Simon & Schuster.

Sunstein, C. R. (2001). *Designing Democracy: What Constitutions Do*. Oxford University Press.

Surowiecki, J. (2004). *The Wisdom of Crowds*. Doubleday.

Tribe, L. H. (2008). *The Invisible Constitution*. Oxford University Press.

Tushnet, M. (2005). *Taking the Constitution Away from the Courts*. Princeton University Press.

Warshaw, S. A. (2015). *The Taming of the Presidency: The Limits of Executive Power*. Routledge.

Wood, G. S. (2009). *Empire of Liberty: A History of the Early Republic, 1789-1815*. Oxford University Press.